GOING BACK

Also By Jim Neely

POEMS
Quarrel In Straw 1972
Pillars 1972
A Partial Victory 1974
Reconsiderations 1976
Blessings 1977

PROSE
Gender, The Myth Of Equality 1981

AUTOBIOGRAPHY
MY Life Before And After San Francisco 2006

ESSAYS
How Your Surgeon Feels 2009

GOING BACK

By

Jim Neely

iUniverse LLC
Bloomington

GOING BACK

iUniverse books may be ordered through booksellers or by contacting:

iUniverse LLC
1663 Liberty Drive
Bloomington, IN 47403
www.iuniverse.com
1-800-Authors (1-800-288-4677)

ISBN: 978-1-4917-1194-1 (sc)
ISBN: 978-1-4917-1196-5 (hc)
ISBN: 978-1-4917-1195-8 (e)

Library of Congress Control Number: 2013919557

Printed in the United States of America.

iUniverse rev. date: 11/09/2013

to Patti

Contents

The Tightrope Worker

Angel in the velvet moon
I cannot catch your eye
you prance such steeples full of fun
your golden scissors two are one
above a deadly sky

unlike below where goad is gain
yours no fear of slip
fatality but finality
cast off with charmer's quip

your high dance begs fear of fail
pure to the joy pursue
O hurry down
teach your weave to us
wink on us anew

end is only end itself
whatever you chance to do

Swinging with Heather

The laughter that fun-curdles your tummy
turns your sky forever into my love lap
will always own the stretch of clear blue
you've learned to seek
with your head thrown back
against the wind
yours is this everlasting gem
to tell the world you better be a better place
than he has lived this past century
as with your smile
a sway pendant of truth today
my tear-dusted face
suddenly knows
we have already done as much
for you as we can
and what you must find yourself now is unlearned
the opening to those whom else madness
I must trust will swing you
half so well as us

Poppy Is Dead
For Christopher

We explained to him
something might enter to a sleeping bird
catch one wing in a corner
pin him unsuspecting in a cage corner
where his towel had not been responsibly drawn
rip out a socket there cleanly
shearing feathers about
before there was even time to cry out
in the night
shit happens
thin bird blood could seep out
noiseless before we knew it
something escapes
something inside him sated
into the darkness of his life
unaware while the bright plumage left
folded slowly in upon itself breathless
like he found it still this morning
so coldly
he packed all the feathers he could find
in the one best candy box
and beneath his high rope
hung from the useless old split oak by the studio
beneath her spread root he dug him deep
a cover with the finest granular glass around
and from the swing circling above
smiling overall he cried
rest down there all of you
your crazy peace

A Farewell to Arms

In the dreary Idaho winter
a man at the one grocery store
there in Ketchum
gave me a lead pipe scraper and told me
you're still young enough
you can maybe probe him
in this blizzard we're having
the great man lay somewhere near
the back cemetery
across from Baldy Mountain
so he can watch the skiers
cosseted by two small cedars

I went the worst day the worst winter in years
six-foot ice drifts covered the stones
you brought one up
flat slabs impossible to read
names all frosted
I chipped and picked layer after layer
double-blind sweat and sleet
double-blind fighting the challenge
be strong
I said
like he wanted me to be
true cool in adversity
for hours slab after slab till finally
one came up ILLER followed by INGWAY
through the ice

I got a picture to prove to you
back at the hotel
my wife wanted to know
was his middle name Killer
no Miller
I said
I think
collapsing both of us in love
dead to the world

Ingénue

In the days before girls
when they needed a part
like in Shakespeare
I was always the one
lithe and lissome schoolboy chosen
nor was I
lost for performance
in fact I put my woman picture
on my desk signed it
With Love From Beatrice
so convincing all
agreed I had some
sumptuous girlfriend
this got serious later
when dressed in cancan fop
it got out the hometown rotogravure
look that's a star there fussing up
our boy's black garter belt backstage on Broadway
imagine my father's relief
unbounded joy
when he found me enthralled
peeping on our nice neighbor lady
undressing one Friday night
with her upright nabob
all sweet to love her

Dancing Class

Every winter Friday night age of ten
regular as rain
we went to the club on Front Street
to learn the waltz fox-trot and Lindy hop
I was in love
I read the Bible before going
to be good enough for her
she had lustrous black hair
wore a black velvet dress with white trim
and smiled as if she
knew something more than I did
even when she really didn't

later when I danced Broadway
I discovered
women sweat
never smile in practice
and there is no lucky spot dance
where if you are there when the music suddenly stops
you will get a prize
contrived by our mothers

it was best of Broadway
you had already had
true love
love of the purest kind
love of the moon and the stars
young love
that can last all of you
a lifetime

Honeymoon

Our flock of white doves always fly
a perfect union
except once a year in late March
when the river herring run
they break formation to fend for themselves
diving the water in a frenzy
feeding on anchovy from a distance
you can see them hone and strike prey
with astounding accuracy
as once fishing off Papeete
on my honeymoon
the captain watched
through binocs to spy
a pelican dive
and knew right off there
that was the place
and we chased over ocean a mile to catch
a deadly peck mark still on its side
a baby dolphin who turned
the most beautiful colors
of the rainbow
dying
there in the boat
my wife four months pregnant crying
as we watched
the shivers came slowly to an end
in the warm sun off Papeete
just like that marriage
twelve years later

The Liberation

She was always there with her smile
no matter what I needed
or took to her for process
no matter what had to be done
when she had her place nearby
we always talked of her children
the little boy was eight
and always hid behind the counter
from me and my smile
imagine my surprise today when
Adrienne came out from behind all those boxes
in her new place
to smile at me with a big embrace
the benefit of her magnificent breasts
a kiss that could launch a lifetime
it was like the GIs reception in Paris in WWII
and when she said that little Luis
was eighteen now
into music
and you should see some of the
unbelievable stuff he brings
into my kitchen
he calls girlfriends
I knew for sure then what a wonderful
woman she had been since I last saw her
all these years

Pitchfork

We would lie on the grass in the dark
after the luminous fireflies
in September when
school was about to begin
shooting stars were angels' frolic
he said and lightning their hunger pains
in central Pennsylvania
lying on your back with your own father
looking up was the best place
the best place in the whole wide world
to see them as light traveled faster than sound
right there where you could clearly see it
could count the seconds between flash
and thunder multiply by this magic factor and find
how miles distant was any storm so you
would always be safe from lightning

even today I wake up
trying to count a storm way out over the Pacific
trying to judge her distance
recall a factor that won't arrive anymore
there is no lightning synapse

strikes come not from a distance
another close friend today
one after another suddenly
gone

Sushi

On a clear flying day
after the grape harvest
I walk alone in peace to the river
at flood tide
overhead young Japanese
airline pilots are practicing
takeoffs and landings at our small airport

when they make their turn and circle overhead
I note beneath their wings
a red square
no cherry spot or rising sun
their noise remains frightful then
disappears over the mountain where
for a time it is quiet with the soft lap
of morning water
a few fishermen quietly tethering bait

these pilots are neighbors
we play bocce ball together
eat sushi for their three months of training
each perfects here before
going home to bigger things
leaving me to wonder why
at my age I still look up at their silver wings
and scared yet
cease to remark
to wife and child
the color shape noise and recognition
of what all of us once
were taught to be afraid
and watch out for

The Mint Doctor

The US Assay office
where coins are still made
and sold to collectors
thinks profit
the only branch of government that
actually makes money
needed a doctor once a week
to clean up their metallic problems
nurse—wonderful D—used to undress
and set up forty female physicals Wednesday
and off we'd go

you ask
was there any romance doctor
you see so much
you'd never know it from me at the time
but yes sure once
I got called after hours
a house call somewhere
a loft in Chinatown
she said she had placed a strand of pearls
in herself
merely wanted me to extract them slowly
like a procedure an operation you know
one at a time
she said she was practicing a rehearsal
for a dance you wont forget
we counted them together forty-four
which she said
meant virility and good luck
for the coming year

sending me out that fast
but later I heard
the pelvic scan sealed her fate
caught trying to exit pieces of eight

Rust

Of all things you can get
with enough mileage
in this world
who would have thought
the living end could be
manhood
as he ages sometimes
whether he has had too much of
a good thing or too little
when he comes for you
the one he loves
its not nothing he has done
even if old girlfriends sitting there
watching the fire go out
are laughing at
old blood suddenly found in his seed

that old goat
serves him right they are thinking
its only that he may bring rust to your love
he doesn't mean
which is no more to worry about
the doctor said today
smiling wear and tear
its just that in some ways
its in bad taste

La Belle Dame Sans

He returns just to let me know
in person
like a man he says
yet he needn't
his pale face
says it for him
all love has gone
she was working beneath the radar
and Dad did this ever happen before
I mean what did people do
and my own hurt
a pain so long ago
bursts open
bleeds all over me again
for the truth of it
for the both of us
crying
hugging there at the airport
my son
home again
just today
heartbroken

Swan Lake

The Black Swan pas de deux
me high on point again
my love of dance
every step along the way
the very its-a-dance of it
I told myself to go backstage after
embrace that young woman
get a signet pose to show off
friends back home
which cost knowing
the sad loneliness of her tears
the execrable yellow stain
of her unhappy life
of which on court today
why was all I said was
and here's us the two of us just smiling there
pictured between sets
me arm in arm with this cool ballerina
in old St. Petersburg

Vickie's Stylish Umbilicus

What she's giving out this year
is the barest slice
of abdomen
where a button rendered useless
by birth
now finds itself fashioned
in the lap
of season
with bangles and ringlets
bedecking
a beacon of love
once nothing much more
going on for her
down there
than a lonely recess

Broke

You want to run
North say to the lakes of Minnesota
open a bait and tackle shop
teach continuing education
to the Zuni or Kwakiutls
at the bottom of the Grand Canyon
maybe a tentmaker
itinerant like Saint Paul
going from Philippi to Ephesus
always on the move
in jail once maybe
twice roving here and there
but spreading the word a good Christian
always ahead of your creditors
or I could be a long bowman
at Agincourt or Culloden
with Pettigrew's Division on
Pickett's left the third day at Gettysburg
lift Dame Margot Fonteyn's skirts
high in the lights like dancer Nureyev
arm rigid beneath her
warm buttocks to great applause
Carmen Nigro working inside Kong
Cushing brainy with a knife
Joan d'Arc in the Movement
Wallace Stevens making nothing of a Snow Man
so much for the pocket nerve
firing off complaints
to accounts receivable
the balance of my day

Her Biopsy Report

Doctor it was like
I was in a field
and in this field I am young again
my washed chest warm in the sun
as this huge eagle wants me
falls exactly gripping both sides
he takes me high with his wings
up out over blue water
talons fast to my stretched breasts
my head goes back
I feel the click of his tongue at my ear
his quick breath
feathers beating up my legs
his claws tremble
till one side is loosening
he can't keep purchase
more clawing wont hold
one side is not enough
he spins away
hopeless
I go down crying
holding up to him a cold arrow
scroll for answers
his sharp beak twists above me
face shroud in black
hooded over this olive I have
growing deeper
and still deeper down
into my heart flesh and blood only
now to discover
you tell me benign
it was nothing at all

First Overnight at Gramps

It's years and still you lie there
watching the curtains move
the fog sweeps in
to cool your sweaty covers
and you hear the same animal noises
yours made
weeks home from the hospital
all of it coming back as if
it were yesterday
the little roots and snorts
muffled cries driven deep into
the pillow of her crib that hurt
and make you jump up
sleepless at a moment's notice

and there she is
bobbing her wide blue eyes all night
in the strange moonlight at some
shadow you dont even know
exists in your own house
you try to love your crying wife back to sleep
from saying
what if she wont even be here alive
for us anymore
when our children return
from their overnight

The Greatest Generation

It was always July burnt to a crisp
our fathers worried
the radio men in brown shirts
burning books somewhere over there
but above all was sun through our sycamore
the springhouse where the boat was hooked
the swimming hole where everything drips sweet
hummingbirds nosing into honeysuckle
frogs leaping
turtleheads bobbing
little raisin heads in seaweed ready for my dash
the quick peel down
the woolen trunks always with a white belt
too big for you
sticky off your sweaty thighs
the high leap
grasp Tarzan's monkey swing that carried you
way out over rippling crags
above the silver waterfall
and back again dangling screaming
help
bloody murder
before right on target
suddenly you let go and plunge
cold
naked
deep
into the cool water
summer paradise enough
to capture what
you would fight for forever after
whenever you got the call

A Sight to See

The four-hundred-pound woman
in the doctor's waiting room
who opens her blouse
flops out a watermelon
to nurse a five-pound premature
while her teeny Hispanic husband
hides his red face
pretending to read
the sports section next to her
upside down

Déjà Vu

You see someone strange
coming at you suddenly
in the park
who appears exactly like someone
alive again you once knew inside out
at a time when
if she saw you now
wouldn't recognize you
as you would seem different to her
but the way you see her now
her features perfect for
that young time together
make you want to
make more sense out of how
it turned out that it never did
when you knew each other
in a way we thought we knew
that depended as much
as anything else could
on the way we looked
to each other
for life and love of one another
and everybody else
at that time
but whats left to say
about all that
to her again
today

Going Back

How do I message your machine
it's fifty years ago today
on the soft green fields above the Hudson
this brevet colonel of the USAF
struck a cleat so deep
with mud above my right eye
that years later
the first husband of Ingrid Bergman
who was trained to wire and screw teeth
but switched to neurosurgery
had to clean out all the bone
fashion a metal plate with fine bolts
into my right temple
removing a huge skull tumor
and part of that same cleat
in order to cover up
an exposed brain

anyway it's Saturday morning again
when I'm required to go yell
and work up headaches over my children
playing at games of soccer to the beach chalet
where nobody believes I have
this metal screw plate in my head from
half a century when I scored
the winning goal against them
all male jocks at West Point

and my team threw cold water on me
as everybody did then
to wake you up
and hoist me high on their shoulders
and ran around the field
shouting triumph with me a hero
held so high to show those guys we won
they could never kill anybody like us like that anymore

so when the hard pains began from babies
tap-tapping my forehead
probing love in my mind's eye
I remembered my sainted father
an ace pilot in France
with the 50th Aero Squadron in the First World War
saying everybody now was going to wear medals
when the Nazis overran Europe
so he sent to collect his Silver Star
wore it secretly behind his lapel
which he could turn out to show dodgers on the street

and suddenly I had to own my medal too
and years later sent for
and sutured lovingly with silk my big Orange P
just for Saturdays like this

but when you go ask them after their game
to feel the screw in your head
they laugh
say yuk
and don't believe

except once in my new sweater at the airport
taking them back to show off my old college room
I couldn't pass the metal detector test
they listened
and wondered why

The Kiss

Believe what you will the holy monks
of Mount Athos Greece lay claim
to the severed left hand of Mary Magdalene beside
a segment of the True Cross whereat
no women are allowed on the Holy Mountain

the men kiss her fulsome hand
they say it is impossibly soft and warm yet
causes them cold tears
wakeful nights and fractured memory

when my father died
my mother told me to go see him
alone at the parlor without the other children
as I was a doctor used to
how it can be once the dead are dead
and I could stand it
while she would have to take the other
brothers and sister in order
to care for their feelings

I saw him there and fell on my knees
to kiss Daddy's forehead so cold
and his head—the head of my father—hard as nails
as my cry went up
and covered his face with a world
warmed full with my tears of love and joy
for him

and never ever after
have I ever had
a sleepless night
or fractured memory
doubting why on earth
of all people
He took my sainted father home

Roses

Looking for the ones to blame
desiring this man's art and that man's scope
going row on row
cutting
slashing
debriding
it comes to me
I am so much part of this world
separating
the red ones from the yellows
the bunches from the loners
a forme fruste here
a robust there
Lucille Ball from the Rose of Picardie
deadheading each
with a
take that you rat
upon arrival

how easy I could be that one there
on the platform
that mad doctor man on the platform
standing uniform erect
as the train stops and people
scared senseless
empty out one by one to hear me
without so much as a word
flick my baton left or right deciding
what good are they good for anyway

if ever I forget
what I have seen this life

The Philanthropist

When I first came to the city
Bimbo's was the place they had this
over the bar this eight by ten inch
small neat little fishbowl full of water
where every twenty minutes
a nude woman swam into view
all the rage

imagine my surprise last night
my neighbor Roxanne
at her party showed me
that very bowl
kept in her closet for half a century
and her picture to prove she was that one
working her way through college

she said did many things barely
even Broadway
and like most things in life
she said it was all done by mirrors
swimming there in a water tank in the basement
for mens jollies

and now when we see her at eleven a.m.
jeweled up in spikes
driving off in her Caddy
to the museum she wants us to know
she is merely giving back to society
what all of us you know
take from it when
we are young

Forbearance

Only later on comes a time
you know what another one
you love is doing
or about to do he shouldn't
you can see it
does no good at all to do
no need to do that in the first place
as you have done it young once
without thinking
anybody then knew
more than you
anything about what you were doing
and it is the same thing now
come round again
this time someone
you love you must allow
the pain of doing
a go-ahead
without saying you already have
a better way
you know of doing that and just how
painless it could be
to get there
in the first place

The Cure

Viral in Ocho Rios
moribund sweats
staring all day
at the white ceiling
a bright green lizard stalks
a white butterfly
as the sun goes down
the colors change
on walls
on the lizard
the flap of butterfly wings
slows and clarifies against
a thin gold shadow
in the coming coolness
my sweat rims quiet at last
coalesce
the fever pitch subsides when suddenly
there at first hand
how a sudden dart
of sticky pink tongue
can shoot out that fast at someone
and kill an entire day

Hot Air Balloon

He started from nowhere from ground zero
took the envelope straight up
riding the high currents
over the mountains
his basket full
of friends waving down at us
a gold balloon colored black
with white highlights
a shimmer of morning light above us
hoping to outrace
a chasing storm
when suddenly
the wind overhead quit cold
there was no place to go
the burner wouldn't lift
there was no control
it came down hard on us
right outside our homes
not knowing what to do
we stared at its magnificence
the lost blossom
the fluttering colors
until the chasers finally arrived
out of nowhere
to put stays on the dome
tethering her while she slowly collapsed
on the street before us
against all our hopes
and those in the basket
on a free ride
forced to land in a place of nothing
but strangers

Doctor Nearly

He came at me by the elevator
pointing his left small finger at me
a hard-on proclaiming
you the man
you the man
the man who did it when I was eight
when I cut off this finger on a toy train
and the dog tried to eat it from the rug
but Mother got it in a jar
and there you were in the ER
when we arrived all ready
to work on me
I watched you sew it on
I remember
you didn't inject Novocain
like most doctors did
which hurts you just slowly
dripped it on till it was numb
from a distance drop by drop
so it didn't hurt like other doctors
I didn't cry
I was so interested
and now I'm a musician
I play guitar
have my own band
and when I reach for a high pick
slide my left up as far as it goes
shake it out and
press it home with your little finger

I always scream YEEOW
that's one for Doc Nearly
for thirty-five years I never forget your name
what Doctor Nearly done
did for me
look at that perfect finger
the best

The Sweet Spot

Think of something you could do
you can dress down for doing
do with a moment of discovery
like the wheel or first fire
this time it's just a racquet
without greens fees
starting time
lift tickets
black belts
who has beer for bowling
sandwiches for sailing
the kids dont want to go anyway
and out there between perfect lines
you bring back your hand just so
and forward smooth over the top
as a ball curves at you from
a smiling friend
power to power
just see what happens when you hit
that one sweet place that makes the whole world
suddenly full
full of love full as your father's love
when he finally spoke
that last afternoon smiling
at numbers
how our end comes often in threes

three weeks without food
three days without water
three hours in the cold without love he heard
Faulkner and Marilyn had died that week
and said he would make it
a grandiloquent triumvirate
as batting third always had been
for him
the sweetest spot to be

Leda

I don't want to bring this up again
but why is it
old women don't dream of young men
old men do dream of young women we met this time
on a bus to Berlin last summer
she said her boyfriend was a footballer
she was from South London
still traveling the world to learn
with an accent sweetened by oooos
at the Jewish museum she bought a book
called *Auschwitz*
and asked me to explain it
as she had heard some history was made there
she had blue eyes and light hair
and looked up to say
you are a mind fook
a real mind fook
you know
my friends talk about really knowing means
not always having just
a footballer fook you so I want to get you
to put on me your knowledge with your power
it would be a change fook for you too

I thought back to the early days of heart transplants
losing patients right and left
night and day
the sadness
the awful sadness
coming out that door in a mask to have to
tell a mother still trembling with hope
to her face
we had lost her child on the table
and yet heroics drove those days
us sworn to care
for the human heart all the heartaches
to start it and stop it and mend it well enough
to go on yes it was
a scaffolding for the heart we built
that endures
a knowledge I told her grander
than what she had in mind for us
as that would be like me at my age
trying to beat the pee out of frogs to raise the dock
which gave her a smile
a sweet satisfaction
that won't go away
or leave me alone
night after night after night

The Nutcracker Again

O body swayed to music
O brightening glance
How can we know the dancer
from the dance
W.B. Yeats, "Among School Children"

This year it will be different
we are told the grand girls
will no longer be just mice
they have been promoted to Cossacks
once their part appears
the costume scrumptiousness
music for the ages
it gets to you again
maybe you are ready for something
the four cygnets in *Swan Lake*
doing their interlocking
sixteen pas de chats
coming down stage at you with smiles
you want to love every one of them
flawless sixteen cat-jumps count 'em
the crowd goes wild
but no . . . not yet
they still look at each other
for what to do next
and you still know your dancer
not the dance

A Soft Shoe for Maybelle

The reason I was late to do your surgery
was the dance I did in the shower
for my dead friend Belle
who applauded so I had to encore
it was the slide out she used to like
when I would slip one cat foot before
then behind going lateral
with the finger snaps the soap makes
before my great sweep and turn
my friend's neck hanging down there
half dead from nerve degeneration
always hung smiles of delight
drooling a groan of approval
no clap but
O how she tapped with her feet
the rhythm-bent knees urging me on
shuffling back her years
I supposed to childhood
each month took a little more
the muscle mass arms and legs
the swallowing ones
speaking ones
all the outward things
the inward still intact
and for two years she kept that rhythm
the one thing she had was rhythm
pounding of the soul
pounding of the heart always there

and to the end
I stopped every week
in my impatient surgical way
bringing my silly ways about getting things done
making a difference
thinking to change life a little
and she shook her head no
nodding at my feet
and each time we danced a little

me with my feet
my neat little lateral shuffle and smile
snapping my fingers in her face
she pounding her legs
more feeble each time
and slowly another friend was going
taking with her my wife's young ways
and my last high idea of care
but the dance comes back
and the rhythm stays
and this morning before the world was awake
in the great quiet light of dawn
alone I danced
in the soap of my shower
just for my old friend Belle
and we laughed and cried again for each other
maybe much too long
that's why I was late for surgery

For Patti Hospitalized

Remember that time at Wawona
we went swimming naked in the cool September lake
that other couple
the corpulent woman with the huge globular breasts
floating after her like errant jellyfish
her stick of a husband with the teeny membership
with straight black hair
straight arrow each side of him down there with a
solitary Chinatown curl at the end

we marveled how people ever coupled
actually got together
me forty-eight
you twenty-two
obscene
why he's more than twice her age
worse than that Picasso man rocking the cradle
but thirty-five years now
five children
us eighty-three and fifty-seven
so everybody finds it fine
saying things like
he's no longer twice your age
twice you would make me one hundred fourteen
even though the interval is the same

so it's okay they say
it's called lovers' logarithm
you catch up
we don't need your calculus
I tell them
we need you

get well my love
we're going swimming
once again

First Responder

She picked me out of a crowd
today saying thank you
I was the one she remembered
the only real one face
she remembered
from all those people's faces
she heard around her
who helped her that time
and she shook my hand good and firm
looking straight at me
so I knew it couldn't be any stroke left in her
but whoever this was
what it meant for me
to greet her tears
her thankful clear blue eyes
was how was I to recognize another
bloodied old face
on the street
ashen when we turned her over
no carotid or femoral pulse
I pounded her chest
started her heart and lungs with know-how
then watched them haul her away out of there
from me
only a month ago
thinking surely this one was on her way
ending up brain dead
here she is thanking me
a fucking miracle

Low Impact

Pecs
lats
quads
abs
pull and push
stretch and stab
abs
pecs
lats
quads
think of muscles as your gods
quads
abs
pecs
lats
getting closer to collapse
lats
quads
lats
pecs
you have sublimated sex

The Leaves

Yet they kept at it so long
so long as they could I guess
long as they seemed to want to
and once we found them
brushed the late fall away
there they were
a miracle
together even as she always said
we know you four kids heard our arguments
silly fights over goods
oh how I hated your father's high road
your men's abstractions
but we knew then what
you could never know till now
how what you've done was part our love
and so we remained
to lie here together
still parents
beneath
his Celtic Cross
at last
for you

Send-Off

Today the good news
I will have all my teeth
until I die
if I get burned or wasted
they can still identify me for rites
my first wife died last week
her friends came to say
its so sad
because its the first one of them to go
and they'd never thought before
what becomes of us
mostly they've discovered the Buddha
though they admit its not the best story
going around out there
his heaven is all in perfect living right here
which makes me
by their lights
one who wants to pray for
whats happening to her right now
decidedly uncool

For George

Today when June called
I knew I hadn't made it in time to tell you George
you were the one who stopped
my children from crying every time I sewed up a laceration
your cases in the next room
always kept so quiet
while mine screamed bloody murder
me the mean surgeon at work
but then you showed me
how to drip the Novocain into wounds
from the syringe needle held high
a distance so the babies could see
the harmless little drops falling slowly
one at a time
benign
clear like raindrops into the wound
having them count each drop
twelve
seven
eleven
nine
me telling stories of dogs and cats I'd fixed up
right there in that same bed right in the ER
little brothers and sisters miraculously saved
rumpelstiltskin
Madeline
Goodnight Moon
all the while dripping
dripping
not the hurtful wound injections I once did
so I tried your
drip
drip

drip
technique
without ever injecting again
and became the miracle man
el maestro of the ER
with happy children
consolable mothers
a smile on the baby's face
in the room next to you
doctor making everything all better
peaceful and quiet
and O yes yes yes
sure sure sure
sure sure sure
and all this hoo-ha George
just because of you this hoo-ha
because we love you and wont forget

Sunday

Our pure white Estrous angel cat
used to lick
only things pink
one winter
between the death of Domitian
and the accession of Commodus
she hit on camouflage
a Finnish soldier
in the Russo-Finnish war
to deliver a brown dove of peace
through the kitchen window
where with time to kill
worried it so
her taste for strawberry sundae
melted away forever

At the Tollbooth

HO HO HO the pelican
whose beak can hold more than his belly can

just long enough into winter
when colors become her most
and the updraft rides easy
into a clear cold sky
the same five or six of them
get together and decide it's time
nothing else matters
but soaring you can do
in the soft high winds
in the still air above
HO
HO
stop-and-go traffic
inching to work
on the Golden Gate Bridge

The Rose Bowl Parade

There must be more that meets the eye
since all the noise that makes them go
is run at them from just below
where a thousand horn men bleat and blow
the bunting high
though nothing's said
they want to prance upon my bed
shellacked nipples perfected
the white boots click to the white-toothed sky
backwardly enough to pry
a groin press of secret promise
beneath around and within pajamas
must be virgins on parade
else who could make my wife afraid
for any game she ever played
to act so funny
youth can run and hop
be even runny
just to want to win today
and so they pause in underclothes
destinations undisclosed
each with a stick of stars to twirl
and queue and step right out as girl
in attitude so parchment literaldaughter
don't strike contemporaneously clitoral

The Church's One Foundation

Speaking of an afternoon to the ladies
of the First Presbyterian Church
over peach cobbler tea
I told them hymns were poems and poems
all good poems were not made of adjectives
but nouns and verbs in action

they said
here is the hymnal
and gave it saying verily
you'll have to prove us
as we have been singing these hymns
most—if not all—our lives
and so with pain at the wrist
where once nails were
driven twixt radius and ulna
to ice the median nerve
I closed my eyes and opened
the Presbyterian Hymnal
to 442 where
blessings be to all the saints
we sang but two verses as
only one adjective descended and even that
by God was
holy

The Leak

If you had a mind of rain
the power in such small drops
to shut down airports
stasis up Fifth Avenue
drive lovers inside
to bed where she knew
it was a bad time
without protection
the very power to postpone night games four hours
when you have to fly to Cleveland
for a makeup game early next morning
cause mudslides in South San Francisco
drown crops in Kansas
flood death in the bayou
depress actors, politicians, gays, all the ships at sea, and
    business girls
who don't want to have to jump puddles to get to
where they're supposedly going
thus thinking of all the worlds perversions
Mr. Rain you're capable of then

why on earth would you settle for
fashioning a drip in anyone's place
good for at least three years and so occult
nobody but nobody cares
if they fail to find just whereat
it comes from except you
the owner

Once

In our middle ages
I sat next to this lady at the
Buena Vista bar in San Francisco
flipping pages of *Anthropology*
look here
she said
young women faces are
so open kind friendly warm
old men so lined with wisdom care love
now turn this page
look
see how fierce warlike scared young men
faces are
look here
how old women are
suspicious, withdrawn, dried prune, native witches
now you tell me
is this all testosterone
poisoning or what
doesn't the world seem like
wouldn't it go best for all
of us having
young women concert
with old men

so the two of us
well out of it
spent the night alone sleeping
off and on
together

Taste

Chacun a son gout
said the old lady
as she kissed the cow
was my mother's favorite expression
as she talked on forever
insisting you never shut yourself up
somebody has to say shut up
to shut you up with punctuation
or the Dow can render you
hit eleven hundred all-time high
as it did that day they found her in the tub
with a gone bottle of Gilbey's
and kindly signed her out
respiratory arrest
breathless
we distributed her rings
which we had always thought
were worth something
only to find
how dead
silence can become of a sudden
all over the world

Ham

Last night I dreamt my brother
was alive with meningitis
I was next to him with my mask on
he needed me
just like when he died five years ago
from a broken heart
on his deathbed singing
somewhere there's heaven
how high the moon
somewhere there's music
how faint the tune

I kept a dream book once
took it to a psychiatrist
who said I didn't need it
but an analysis would be great fun
for both of us

three years later we were friends
drinking together one night
he said I had taken his chair by mistake
that very first day
we sat down there
in his office
so it was
he continued
an unusual arrangement
which leads me to know exactly what
Jamshid would say of Ham's dream this morning
like a good psychiatrist
nothing

The Clocks Bar

I went to fetch my brother again
from staring down the black
sands of the world
the hourglass blur of Bangkok to Berlin
mirrors twirling
Moscow
Manila
Tel Aviv
Toronto
twirling time all around the world right there
he was all-night bleary wants me
to drink on with him at nine a.m.
I looked beyond for once
said I got a life
didn't he know by now
all those faces screaming
life is short
not to waste it
I can no longer be your fucking keeper
we cried
his from drink
mine from my last shot of care
for a genius whose
ticking brain
had to get much worse
to want help
but enough had gone for
me at last
to leave him there alone
and walk away cold
out of his life
for good

Molly

She circles endlessly
speaking morning
the proposition of being alive
and when the sun comes north
just right
beaming hope
through the window
the first hints of spring in the valley
she settles for comfort
on my lap
stares up at me
a perfect sunbeam
silent without using any forebrain
as she knows I will attribute all kinds of qualities to her
I endue beautiful women
qualities that don't in fact exist
enduring love, romance, unselfishness
it's a character weakness
I must guard against all
my life and goes on
until the pressure becomes
unbearable and I must get up to urinate
relief—I imagine—to both of us

The Cardboard Slide

Every fall they cut out their own idea
of perfect squares
and we would take them
to the hills high above the Presidio
where the wild summer rye lay
brown and smooth
against the slope
and they would slide all afternoon
in the autumn sun
hunched together
all the way down to me
catcher at the fall line
roaring and laughing
to be gathered up victorious
safe in my arms
until men came saying tomorrow
we plan to prune these edges
build models
save a newt or two a species
found only here
you know
hereabouts in all the world

when our hill was already just right
brown and smooth
a child's perfect cardboard day
to slide down
forever

Their New Chem Teacher

The boys had their coordinates
they called them
fixed in stone
for what was already known to come
and it was not until
she took them to another place
for the expanse of their minds
she said
how her special reagent
could change an ordinary glass of water
sitting there on the sink
all by itself suddenly green to red
in what she called
a no-shit moment
that they got together and agreed
not only did she not have
pretty good coordinates in herself
but she gave a whole new meaning to
what they now could call
without stretching themselves too much
fantastic moments
to look forward to
in her chemistry to come

The Burden Lesson

When migration time comes
the tribeswomen fill their waistbands
toting immense gourds of water that
bear them down to run far behind the hunters
at a distance they can barely see
but as the hunt goes on
with providing
their supply grows less and less
the burden lightens
water dwindles
the waistbands let go
empty gourds are thrown
and at last they can stay close to the fight
with their men
but they say when you ask them
even when they are finally free
they are not so happy
as at the beginning
when they are laden
with the burden of giving
away to all the others
what each of them needs to survive

My Feminine Side

At first it is not their bodies
the small things made them happy
a restaurant corner where you
could look only at her
so she could face out on the crowd
to be entertained
walks along Lake Mendota
you must keep the water side
for her safety
holding hands with another
yours had to be
always the one in front
a million things like this
to remember each night
gives me hope for their
happiness as loves we all loved long ago
have long been loving others
and do they remember as I
the little things
count their names as I still do in order
to sleep

it's not until I fall to oblivion
perhaps to dream
Rhoda arrives clutching
both her young breasts just at that moment
she is about to get her gun
ululating
Sweet Jesuses from the recesses of her
extenuated neck that I
wake up acutely
undone with my life
everything else about me
back when

Up in the Old Hotel

He got up
didn't he
he dressed himself
buttoned all those three gold buttons
insinuated himself down the stairs
opened the door
came out
sat down on the bench with his chin resting
square on his one gold cane
to feel the sunrise over the tenderloin
watch the stoplight glare
green to yellow to red
in frenzied commute
inching downtown
and just as we STOP count the seconds
he reaches down with one deft hand
to crease his captain's pants
and smile a smile half
a paralyzed face
to tell us something
we all should know by now
in order to go on downtown to work

To Vivian Gone

Mother-in-law
arrived in a cloud of dust
know-it-all who knew everything
who visited early on
to say with curled lip
you think you are perfect
don't you
when all I ever wanted was to set
a place before us
just so we could both always eat together
but it got worse and worse like the time
on the Golden Gate she directed me
to get sex on the side
it's good for both of you

but Vivian
even you changed to discover
it was your own daughter
who did the breaker
in the dream house no less
I was building all for her
and suddenly you became the woman
you in fact always were the soul of woman
keeper of the keg
with kindness and care
in all those after years filled with
fun and love beyond imagined
as if to make up forever
for two mistakes you once made
one with me
and me with her

Opening Ceremony

Across the river
the red airport lights cease
to blink their nighttime warning
as over the meadow
a flock of a thousand white doves in perfect ceremony
appear released to circle the rising sun
above the stadium with their message
whiter than the underside of avocets
ospreys herons or pelicans
than plumage of the egrets
neck of the eagle
and coursing far above the illegal geese
who cease to gaggle momentarily
and keep their probe to themselves
to look up at the spectacle of peace above
as in the distance from the trenches across the way
the song of a solitary soldier sings his clarion call
for the twenty-four-hour truce as Christmas comes down
for the whole world out my window
before the children arrive
once again

The Barges

They were always there for us
out our boyhood window
fighting the current
the mile-wide Susquehanna
pushing aliquots of coal
and where they came from
or where going to
made no difference
to me and brother Ham
when we could bet their races
as their aft paddle wheels
whirred dripping water
pushed a barge of shiny
anthracite across up or downstream
above the dam
that held back water enough
to make the broad sweep
out there just deep enough
for flat-bottomed boats to churn
the channel
we liked best when two or three of them
lined up
struggling endlessly
even to make no headway
in the strong spring currents
as that seemed to us more like real life
our fight that would go on forever

Entropy

It's has been happening all along
since birth
each living crescent we aspire
once necessary
turns out never to have been so
in the first place
our grip on the summit gives
release with resignation
to what's handed down to us
by the helix of others

complaining about that even today was a friend
who had all the world
blushing with fame
who looked me square in the eye crying
to allow that hills are forever
templates to rest our heart against
the truth of what you do
no matter where you go
you take your slippers off each night
to the same old sinful self
a soul struggling against itself
and tides go on each morning
seasons chase a ring
and less less less less sleep brings

Day Of Infamy

The avocets are here again
perched high
on long, lazy grasshopper legs
white patches on forehead
yellow-orange bills
black and white wings
white eyes
they occupy my still pond this morning
scooping sleepy brine shrimp
with carefree upturned bills
just as a flight of zeros leave their eaves
gather a swallow formation
sharp wings
forked tail
piercing cries
they come in from the northwest
out of the sun
climbing high and screaming
dive down
on a Sunday morning
ridding the pond of all civilization
before church

Yellow Rumped Warblers

If it weren't for their tactile jaundice
I don't think I'd be at this now
but by God there they are
by the bucketful
debriding the punch list
on our grand old olive tree

for those who never remodel
a punch list is all those little things
your friendly carpenter forgot to do
a swatch of red here
a john handle there
things he thinks are just gelding the filly
and never get done

and so it is with these late bloomers
just when our masterpiece
has given forth its last January
grasp of lush ripe green olive plops
for martini lovers
here come the minor surgeons
picking away at zits and pits
mangling branch over branch
noisily shrieking their collective
yellow bird ass
unalterably opposed to any winter rest
for all of us at all
who are left alone now
fending for the ages

Awakening

This morning
with the cats still warm in my bed
and the sun just up over the Napa River
through the fog
and a wedge of Canada geese framed for me
going north out my window
a blue streak of jet far above
crosses the winter sky toward LA
where my five children are likely still sleeping off
young love's frustrations
and as the fresh rosebuds in the patio are
promising spring again
A's pitchers are reporting
this very first day for spring training in Arizona
that will give me something to do all summer

I promise myself
I will not count the friends who have gone on
nor the lovers I've had
who left me for someone else
nor count them ever again as I did last night
one by one
when I couldn't sleep

rather will I get up and walk down by the river
to see the new cement circle theyve made here
where I live at last
with every member's name on it
I will admire the patience of fishermen
across the way
and if I can
I will find God again in nature
and I will try to understand once more
how death is the mother of all this beauty

Mileage

Imagine my surprise after dinner
out on the patio
watching September good-bye
when my wife approached
from behind
and cupped my
new breasts
budding like
schoolgirl erasure tits
from old man loss
of testosterone
with her whispering love
in my good ear how
I now know just what
you felt like
feeling me up
all these years

Mercy

The Hippocratic face looks up at me
from a crib
me who is licensed in pain
the small curled hands extend punctures still oozing
her ashen face feints a smile at the life drips
coming in clear through a tube
I twist a paper tape
stick it on my nose
give a clown laugh
looking up
she breathes her last gum-grey smile in short coughs
points to her own
I fix another
slowly twirl it
place it smack on the tip of her nose
funny clown
she laughs
funny funny
I blink back tears
I cannot see
the sun slant lowers her railing
what must I do
cause no pain
they taught me
the experts are all gone again

alone
I hold her hand
cold blue clammy
blind I reach and squeeze the pinchcock into my heart
watch the drops cease
leave the room
smiling at the parents with my face

Fall Gathering

For talk we never watched the game
I said Lear's Cordelia did love him
only couldn't say so
stop looking for a sign stop pacing the shore you guys
just allow your progeny their own life
and afterward what remains of us
sang the old songs when lyrics mattered
that time arm-in-arm
when Toe was still alive
a voice so sweet and clear
we got laughing
over an empty keg his line
she's swell as the Brooklyn Dodgers
she peps up the oldest codgers
and while it was still early
enough sun over the bowl
to see our way
whats left of us
left each other again
home to bed
wives half our age
who wander year after year
what's all the fuss about

How Life Begins

Even when they are going for the gold
doing triple this
double axel that
whatever her edge
here with a third wife
at seventy a man still sits
checking out
what of her
colors and vines
figure access
when she is all stretched out down there
before him
on ice

Cobweb

Just when you want to catch up
only in briefs
whats above the paper fold this morning
the August sun setting up
bright colors on six hot air balloons
making their way down valley
low riding today in kindly breeze
enough to see this august turn of year
red grapes full to bursting
our schoolchildren berry brown out
at summer's end
a leg up on school already
so they can have their ski week in February

I lean to the driveway for my read when
suddenly a cotton net closes down my face
coming from the sheltering birch
that hides me from the neighbors
an overnight workout no doubt
His Majesty Arachnida
lying in wait for me there
hidden deep among the branches
waiting for the slow strangle of
Gulliver tethered and caught here
with my pants down

January

The children have gone
wherever it is they go now after holidays
I step outside
my arm around my wife
still weeping
in the night
in the still cold air
I look to say how the water in the river slows
high slack tide now just as it did when my Susquehanna
as a boy I watched from my window
how she slowed to form the big ice chunks this time of year
which froze her amazing journey to the Chesapeake
the Atlantic
the whole wide world

as from the coastal mountains
a mile away
a lone she-wolf cries up
to an imperfect moon shrouded in mist
her mother plea
for all mammalian biology why
on earth
this pain as if
her only child has been lost to her
taken away tonight
parted forever

On Yeats's Tower

Go north out of Gort
the best right you see
the narrowest branch
that's Thoor Ballylee
support your hand
on the smooth cold stone
that winds up to parapets
of Yeats' young home
there feel the wind
blow clean on your ears
face the four ways
he did for years
north toward Sligo
where Drumcliff Church rests
and horsemen still pass
ignoring his death
east to the Abbey
in damp Dublin town
where repertoire thrives
and buses go round

south to Coole
the swans in the park
Lady Gregory's ruins
light Ireland's dark
and west to the ocean
the brave came across
American gyres
fill Ireland's loss
an ocean to keep
and span once again
as long as words
make distinction in men
as long as he said
there's a world of pity
at the heart of love
in every big city
cast his cold eye
on mourning ablutions
life is a process
look out for solutions

Ellendean

That day Patti was all alone
grief stricken
when her brother chose a bridge
our adopted West Coast
Grandmother suddenly
appeared with paper and crayons
assigned each child a room to draw
their favorite animal
without a word
took her to the dining room
told her to sit down
take off her shoes and stockings
and crippled at eighty
Ellendean kneeled down
before her crying eyes
with soap and warm water
to carefully wash her feet
and tell her whenever
somebody dies you feel better
when you kneel and wash the feet
of someone you love

Encore Paree

With you I'll go back to Paris
if Paris is still the same
saucers piled high on Montparnasse
books along the Seine
accordions down the Metro
mon Tabac dans l'Odeon
puppets in the Luxembourg
l'Etoile in the sun
lovers loving the Ile Saint Lou
painters up Montmartre
that carousel in the Tuileries
children who break your heart
the mimes outside the corner eglise
the flame beneath the Arc
Winged V. as you hit the Louvre
Les Deux Magots for a start
just maybe an old girl in Paris
who said we boys set her free
will still be around in Paris
to call me her one cherie

and here we're again back in Paris
always a sight to see
and I would remain in Paris
if my Paris remained in me

Basic Need

A hundred honkers indian-file
their way across
the meadow to the river
acting as usual why they dislike
each other
complaining
fidgeting up the ass of the one just ahead
to move faster
over a ragged terrain of
hawks, killer rabbits, coyotes
eager to strike any straggler

but soon as they reach the water
fresh in July flood tide with
food and refreshment
each cries out triumphant freedom
relieved to be alone
to go their own way
with the mellifluous flow upstream
until the warm huddle everyone needs
comes quietly again together
against the cold darkness of the night

Beatitude

To walk between
where the tide stretches out
waves toward its apex
before going back
and that of the beach's dry sand
to stay along
the moist firm part where foot
leaves a mark
newly washed shells are
birds find excitement
there's driftwood
and clean bones from the sea
to maintain to weave here a course
in the crystalline wetness
neither up too far or down too deep
in the momentary firm beneath you
is to succeed for once
untempted in sands of the desert
nor yet to walk on water

Jaundiced

Chained to this yellow pad
ironbound Prometheus
vultures tearing your swollen liver
nibbling deadly aliquots
substance of your life
I tell you
you want to die
it's fifty years ago
she said
life depends upon the liver
Mother said that to a child
she drove home from Cape May to Harrisburg
my capitol of Penn's woods
sickly child with summer hepatitis
in her lap I never told her
how she scarred my delicate years to liver failure
the night before in the old Chalfont Hotel
grown-up noises in the next room
that make sex terror to a child
she was dying
Daddy was killing her

I would never have another birthday
up the Yellow Breeches Creek by the weeping willow
with my friends by the dam above the ripples that ran
down to Susquehanna
out to the whole wide world

all these years I could never give blood
they said I was a carrier
from something that happened in childhood
though myself was cured
could go on doing whatever surgery
you want on anybody
except just once catch a needle from this new stuff
some AIDS patient sure as hell
you'll turn yellow again
lie here itching
dark urine
clay-colored stools
anorexic for six weeks
half-alive
half-dead staring
the white walls vacant crazy with the soaps

and think of your mother gone
all the things you could never share
how she cut off your boyhood
when you were young and still loved her
when all you ever wanted from Mother
was to be the love of her life

Mother's love
against the world
that immunity
nobody else could give

Trinh

Widow of war and madness
child of Vietnam who saw
her father killed with a hoe
escaped alone by boat
comes Wednesdays right on time
with rags and mops to work the neighborhood
nothing is too much for her
too small where that face comes from the rice water stools
of Malaysia rats biting the sick to sleep
rubber blood clots big as tires
on a roof in Saigon

she told me how she loved only one man
choked back tears to be quiet
not to be killed herself
as they slit his neck and pithed him
pulled out his spine to die
and yet she still smiles at my grilled TV
bows endless thanks to our gift of freedom
and quietly writes perfect English to a red cross
each night in tears
to her children left somewhere behind

Being Two Places at Once

When I had my dream place at Tahoe
I always worried about my patients
left in San Francisco
and when in SF
I always worried about not using
my place by the lake
Robert Louis Stevenson called
the most perfect quiet in all the world
its funny how my wife still remembers
exactly the blue jays by name
the baby deer
the bears in the yard
squirrels in the tree house
teaching five kids one by one
to swim en été
to ski en hiver
the time I cut down the neighbor's pine tree
I shouldn't have
selfish for our own Christmas tree

while I always remember when
son Robert went off the table edge age three
an avulsion laceration of his right eyelid
holding back blood
with one hand

I drove him to the hospital in a blinding blizzard
sewed him up myself
when the plastic surgeon was stuck in snow
and everyone said it was wrong
to operate on your own child
unethical
you shouldn't sew up your own child
what if something happens
he loses vision sight
how can you ever forgive yourself
wait for the plastic man

Fuck You
I said
and did it myself
and Robert made the mean nurse hold up a mirror
so he could see
each of fine thirteen stitches
in a three-year-old's eyelid
just how you place them
what you do
if you want to be a doctor
he said
grown now to become my cardiac surgeon

Grand Central

To wonder here below again
to remind yourself how forever
going and coming
anywhere is to find
wherever you are at last
is always there to discover
the surprise
there is no change made
in yourself whatsoever
and at least home here is to find people
have plenty of room
right in the center
of a market
enough to spare so as to always appear
to be going nowhere at all
when they really aren't
or at least it's the same slow motion
as in an old 1912 reel
shortly after it opened
and that round information desk still
there center stage
with nobody ever there asking questions
the gold clock within
the exact same time whenever you look
from four different directions
and maybe you are not exactly in
the mansion promised you one day
over the river for good behavior
but surely this is grandeur right here
central to your life
man-made majesty
everlasting

Blackie

It was given out
he had swum the Golden Gate
side to side
south to north
in riptide
before there was a bridge
he had won the bet
then put to pasture
always there on the way to Tiburon
the kids made us stop
every time each time
to pet his nose cush
they called it
as we watched
his rickety back dip down
down
down
down
to the ground

year after year
systems failing by the book
the sex first
the slow water
then breathing
then the heart
the eating less
the hormones lost
to a scruffy coat
and last the nervous system

five senses always last to go
so we can lie there
a wounded animal
seeing
hearing
smelling
touching
tasting hello
to the very end a lump of sugar until on the way
to Tiburon
that long day
he was gone
and my youngest said
the last time he saw him
and petted Blackie's cushion
Blackie told him
not to worry wherever he is
because if he is not just right there when you pass him
he is somewhere near
it is because it is never ever
any end

Pops at Large

The home stretch
golfing miniature
time to bring it
behind the green screen fence
next the freeway zoom
my grandgirls tee me up
my ball sky blue on the inverted scrub brush
I send it rolling
to the yawning dragon maw
whose eyes wobble seductively as I split
her screaming uvula
inside the plywood castle
the wobblies keep going round and round
making guttural thumps
a metronome of slave ship oars
till a ball shoots out now a robin red
accouchement
below the silver falls
spinning across the grey Astroturf
to the gold-haired diadem
pay dirt number nineteen hole
where the fat lady leans back
crotchety
siphoning up
our final run
nor girlhood thoughts
of any fun

The Living End

Every year still under twelve
exactly the last two weeks of August
it was always the Chalfonte
in Cape May where colored people
as my parents called them
up from Richmond
waited tables every Saturday night
when they thought we were asleep
me and Ham would sneak out back
to the slave quarters we called it
to the helps party
where black men now slick in tight white jackets
would dance with trays on their head
filled with rainbow sherbet
while their women in short white skirts
right before our eyes
took off their underthings to dance
the black bottom

once one took me aside
and showed me herself
she said
its where it all starts boy
the living end
which came down all of a sudden
like the very next day
the exodus
right on time
Tuesday after Labor Day each year
and gave me something
to look forward to all year long
dream about coming again for a lifetime

Diva

Alone she presents
herself downstage
before her call
spotlighted
in morning sun
the coldest day
of a new year
January
surrounded
not by the host of golden
she's known for
rather defiant
in a rock garden
in perfect yellow
for the world to
acclaim her first again
the one and only
Daffodil

Sometimes

Sometimes I repeat myself
Sometimes I forget my best friend's name
it's one thing
somebody claps you on the shoulder
you turn and suddenly block a name
thats trouble enough
still its acceptable
there's an excuse
at some parties now everybody gets name tags
even your next-door neighbor
to save you this grief
it gets that bad
doctors call it nominal aphasia
advise you use mnemonics like
two zebras bit my ass for five branches of the facial nerve
I try little reminders like my best friend's name
is like that *Top Gun* movie star
but can't get beyond Tim or Tod Ted or Tad
for weeks
and he won't answer any clue

I think all us in the end
given one wish
would say I wish I could give more
not take so much
but have given more
to the world

so much other is
remembering one with special breasts
another who took your picture
split en face
gross names that did unimaginable seamy
things to your soul

but my last wish would be to remember
all at once
the people who meant so much to me
tell them each by each first name
clear as crystal
how much I love you

Settlers

Here raise a glass to Jack London
who died in a white suit
with his boots on
above San Francisco
drinking in
The Valley of the Moon
who wrote forty-three novels in seventeen years
exploded a meteor age forty
all over the world
yet what is *White Fang* from our childhood
to these small graves
two early immigrants here
next to him
at rest on the hillside
facing the golden sunset
above the Pacific each evening
the great live oaks whispering
all around
these are children
nameless unknown children
without a mark
you sit down next to
on the wet fall ground
weeping quietly for them
alone

Without Children

There comes a sudden shock
when the trees stand still
you hear a whole house
its own soft noise
a silence becoming
a sudden drop from where youve been
with all of them
to where you're sure to go
looking for the surface of waves
maybe just one this afternoon
you could feel the surge beneath
that would take you
the ride down and inward
beyond yourself
carried on its own driven impulse
curling around
to straighten up at last for you
to ride us out beyond
ourselves
just as one close branch stirs
across my window
declaring the world out there
cannot last
without them
and do you ever want it to

Minnie Gates

Up from the Deep South 1930s
she had a six-inch keloid scar on the left side
her face where whites tried to kill her
still with a smile that would stop the world
laughter from her very bowels
rocked the whole house
every day
she taught me
you wipe fore to aft
ring a chicken neck till they no shivers
gut it from above down
same as with catfish bass trout
how to paraffin seal
beans strawberries
stewed tomatoes crabapple sauce jars for winter
and when you get to the White House
for manners she said
they'll serve you from the left
and clear you from the right

her sex lesson was everlasting
women can't hurt their thing
but you men can yours so
beware a women's

I was always hoping Mother
would be at the Library Board
so we could have cone pone
hominy grits, spoon bread fritters, chitlins
shoofly pie, apple pan dowdy

she with such immense mammas
that clasped you
buried you
deep in love so grand
you'd never ever know again what heavenly
paradise was till when
I went back east to mother's funeral there
at the Pine Street Presbyterian Church narthex
there she was waiting for me
fifty years later
Minnie grasped me
smothered me to her big black bosom
crying
oh my jimmie jimmie jimmie
melding us one in the sweetest oily suet
of her incomparable love and joy
I cannot describe forever to you
the words

Purgatory

When I die let me be a standin a while
for the shrunken head kept by
Trader Vic's restaurant
San Francisco sealed
secure against the elements in glass
by the cash register
among the South Seas specie
guns spears shields outriggers
hung from the ceiling
with plum plants and strum music

I wont then have to
entertain my out-of-town guests on so little notice
listening will be predictable as another order
of bamboo shoots and pressed duck
and the endive luncheon ladies
with their comes and goes
can still point out
see how his hair still grows

Game Face

On my way home
just this side of the bridge
a red-tailed hawk holds fast
against the wind and fog
soaring perfectly
wings limp working upwind
tireless with some ancient fix on hunger
his sharp beak mutes time and circumstance
his eye looks down a dim critic on all our plans
stalking a certain kindness
sharp justice in all things
and when finally the descent comes
breaks the silence
the pending darkness gives way
all at once
to the edge of mercy waiting
behind the calm quiet of
the surgeon's mask

Party Pooper

Now that I am retired
people want free advice at parties
like Curt age seventy-five last evening
whispered that boil he had
told me about a month ago
when he stopped me with a cartful
at the supermarket

you know at the base of my spine he said
you know there at the top of my crack
the one my doctor just squeezed
still drains stuff Doc
what should I do

I said it is a pilonidal cyst
you were born with it
believe it or not
you are irritating it riding that damn tricycle
what it needs is real drainage
by an armed surgeon
not somebody who squeezes

as just then his wife overhears me
wants to know if I would do it
drain it on the side at home
she said

and incidentally added
what is your opinion on circumcision
because my first grandson already has one
but now his mother
she thinks the new baby boy due next week
his brother shouldn't be done
its such cruelty to a newborn
or does that make boys fight in the shower
comparing who has the best one

I told her
once I had a patient whose wife
claimed her husband had sparks fly
out his ass during intercourse
I reassured her that
that never killed anyone

with that she scowled turned
and walked away from me
forever

The Trill

On the day Aunt Tweeter passed over
because Tweeter said never say die
we boys on the sidewalk grew sad
as her one beau Earwicker
canary who never sang
all those years
was released to fly free
the great green cemetery
behind our capitol dome

Tweeter
who taught continence always
told us only the male bird sings
and in all species
was the only one capable of truly great art
and then only when deprived of gratification and to see
Earwicker purchase there on the tip of Tweeter's left ear
quietly Cleaning out the brainy recess
of gathered wax was us to know firsthand
man's requited love

a bird of happiness
and when at last
they laid Tweet to rest
from deep in a tree nearby
the most beautiful bird song ever heard
in Central Pennsylvania brought tears
to us few who remained
the few who still talk about
the last mating call of the
the irrepressible Earwick
and cry

Haunted

Even though he said he'd come back
to haunt me
if he didn't survive my surgery
I thought he was gone
for good
once he bled out
died on me on the table that day
unresectable
fifty years ago today
imagine my startle
to see him going round a corner
just now downtown
carrying his three-year-old daughter
over my incision
over his right shoulder
she had red hair
rose freckles a pugged nose
just like him in his last smile good-bye
visit that night before with her
only today she was crying

Envoi

When I first went back to see him
my old professor
I told him how hard it was for me
to teach the new generation of surgeons
to operate

he said it was because
you have forgotten how awful you were
like a cub bear trying to masturbate
with boxing gloves on
when you began

but years later
introducing me to a crowd
he said I had become a great teacher
under his guidance
as at last I had remembered
how bad I was with him
when he began with me

that it is thus in this way
with each generation we all
learn to give ourselves away
knowing our own infirmities
for everyone to see
our complications
we take with us leaving light to others as we go
he said
for them to go beyond us
as in giving ourselves away to them
we gain our own lives
so remember what I said to each of you
he said
about how bad you were
then he died

Denouement

If you must be tall
she said to the end
be tall and stately
like the redwoods at the Children's Library
that grow and grow
as long as you live
point to the heavens

but while my ears do grow
paddles trying to catch
everything you say
and the feet splay out with use
a larger size each year
and the organ of reproduction
won't fool or care to stand up at the party
there is no reaching for stars anymore
Mother dear

nor do any of my sitzmarks you left
chevroned on the doorjamb
trending upward for me to survive
carry any weight
as the grandchildren at the library
now know they are that much taller
are straight arrow already
drawing Godzillas in half the time
a magnificence
of earth and trees surrounded
owning themselves
in the very heart of here and now
where I am no longer tall at all
or hardly ever stately

Harrison Street

Drawn like a magnet wherever we were
from all over the world
whatever we were doing
we always went back there
to the same place Mother complained
Dad's heart raced when he drove up Harrison Street
the battlements
his '17 classmate Scottie Fitzgerald called them
coming at you in the distance
how he'd get chest pain
she worried his heart raced so
as did others no one could understand

but to those of us who were there
après notre guerre WWII
it seemed a place
not like the others
which are never what they are
said to be as this always was
for us that perfect place

I told my son
who took his steady
to show her his own place there last weekend
trying to explain to her what he was feeling
when they drove up Harrison
that all I could come up with
to explain our joy to her
looking back on it

it's what we all knew to be true
when we were young
and in love
and back in Princeton

The Assistant

Imagine me on the other side of the table
seeing you run late
I would greet the room
know which side of the bed each got out
make sure your light was right
fix the drapes
fashion the field exactly
the way you like it
and when you arrive
I will know by the coffee titre on your breath
the fine pill-rolling tremor in your hands
your child had a high fever overnight
your wife's biopsy is not yet back
the lawsuit has come back again
them trying to destroy you

and without so much as a word
know what more is needed of me
to make you look good today
anticipate your every move
be always a step ahead
no matter how much it hurts

we'll bring it home all right
slick as a dick for you
without so much as a curse
word between us
we'll wipe the area clean
the room will fill with restaurant talk
what to do for dinner
where to go for fun
accolades for you all around
and you could be off to talk to the family
consumed in afterglow
another surgical triumph
leaving me alone inconnu
but closing fast on the day, sir
I will not cover your ass forever

The Clot

In the end we take cover in kindness
each a rose patina for all that has happened
but when you still wake up of a morning
wondering why
your first wife you loved
with all the love of first love
who you built a dream house
down by the water for with a kiln
because she loved to pot after school
with our two perfect children
as the sun set gold across the bay
why she was unhappy with me
a man in bed
when she had what I grew up thinking
what I had done
would make any woman happy
to love you what you were doing for them
but unlike other times
you think back on dearly now
even wounds you don't agree to
this is no blister
this runs deep
a clot breaks off again
and she is no longer here
of any help

The Solution

She came at me full tilt
at my brother's funeral
a leaning tower of décolleté
claiming she knew me
more than I could ever imagine
as all she needed to know
my favorite word was commodious
which I had employed
she said
somewhere in my autobiography
describing a woman's breasts and
anybody who could write with such rare insight into
women she found totipotent
and would give anything to know how I do it
as she was taking a course herself
in her off-duty hours as a lawyer to learn

all our writing is different, I remember saying to her
today its potency
so what are you up to my morning miracle
awake
with no solution in hand

March 1941

My father kept a German helmet
shot through and through
in our country place downstairs
on the mantle next to
the Great War propeller
he called it the Dead Heine
and sometimes he would let us
take it down and probe
the wound of entrance and exit
amazed thinking what he had done

during vacations then we stayed at a hotel
the Marlboro-Blenheim in Atlantic City
which was always lit up full of life
people from everywhere
laughing
having the best time

after dinner once
Father took me for a walk on the boardwalk
it was Easter 1941
a band played "In your Easter bonnet with all the frills
    upon it"
when an explosion suddenly lit the night sky
out to sea you could see
a ball of fire maybe a quarter-mile off
high as the Empire State
a tanker—red, white, and blue
split in two

heaving upward agony
then going
down
down
down

we shirked our duty he said
we should have gone to Berlin
now you boys will have to do it was all
he said and shook his head

again and again
as we returned
to the hotel with everything suddenly
shut down
terrified in darkness
scared to death
knowing only
whatever could happen to us now
could come down on us
right here now anytime

The Travelers

Now with nothing but time
they give you the feeling
soon as they come back
they missed something again
and when you reassure them
it was just not what they
thought might have happened here
that the thing missing for them
was not here at all while they were gone
they gasp how then it must be
or about to be somewhere else
other than where they have already been
and so visceral is this must
they turn right around and embark
once more
for what was missed as it
must be further away from here
where it was not
and even though my picture of the Acropolis
is clearer than theirs
though I have never seen it
or that Abraham Lincoln never
traveled further than New Orleans
where he saw live men once
done up on the block enough
to last a lifetime
they're off again
parts unknown
before we could say any
Jack Robinson

Joe

Just when she thinks she knows me
everything about me
after all these years
how a boy needs escape
imagine my wife's astonishment
as we drove past a field
of miniature horses
circus ones at that
in red harnesses and blue head tassels
rehearsing a carousel
to learn I did too have a pony once
Shetland Joe who liked sugar lumps
crab apples peach pits peppermint drops
and required my prompt attention
first light every morning
so he wouldn't get mad
get his nose stuck
in the white fence slats waiting for me
wouldn't scrape me off against our old oak
or crush my leg riding bareback like Jesus
to make the quick getaway
a boy needs every day
from his mother

Spunky

This a.m. there are no ideas
but in my thing the rooster crows
cock-a-doodle-do-any-snatch'll-do
but no can do
God's in His heaven proclaiming
save that spunk
for combat
where you are likely as not
to partner a woman today
who's out there for the exercise
not the game one who'll require you
beyond His first commandment
even though she plays
like old people fuck
like porcupines
to tell her she's wonderful
beyond words
she's just here from Chile
for the weekend crush
of the golden grape season
so make sure she goes home thinking
we all had this wonderful

wonderful time out of the house
alfresco among the vines
away from our beds
in the Californication sunshine
in health and in sickness
death us do part
batting a ball almost back from forth
mad dogs and Englishmen
out in the noonday sun
jouons au tennis
porcupines
on the tennis court

The Interview

To this day who am I
when she had come so far
back east
to dine with me
with a smile destined
for theaters
all over this world
to disclose to her she had
caught from the salad course
a sprig of lettuce
irrevocably gummed
to the upper inner aspect
of her great incisor
while two hours talking
how makeup successfully
covers up
her birthmark on her right cheek
at the angle of her jaw
for close romantic takes
that would remain
a secret she said kept for her
hidden by Hollywood all her life

Au Milieu de La Nuit

When I get up
Molly follows me
in the dark
and stays with me
waiting patiently
without a sound
to the last drop
off the lily
and when we return
to bed together
she waits for me
to settle down
on my right side
till she can join me
to fill the crook
of folded knees
where I am careful
not to attribute
qualities to her
that do not exist
while she shows
the same regard for me
as we fall back to sleep
together again always
without saying
so much as
a word

PSA

Eighty-five this week the time
each yea a man starched white with ready glove
gets at my every access until last year
I got my first practitioner
lady with short blonde hair
all business mouth
one who claimed a gentler insinuation
more local respect than all her male forbearers
for the deep image she
lovingly describes your left and right prostate
she calls prostrate
lobes with tour director adoration
calling forth findings via the educated fingertip
your gland volume this year is oh
around thirty-three grams
maybe fifteen cc left
eighteen cc right
just slightly enlarged normal is thirty
amazing you're so small there for your age
with no dominant masses
she laughs when I suggest
small prostate volume is
a function of its frequency
to be emptied

she whispers someone should do
a study as she knows of none such
I suggest we start one together
the larger the prostate the more the pity
by which lights she smiles
to pronounce me good for
another ten thousand miles
pending my morning blood work
my real numbers
to come

Wake

The grasp and hold
of an old lady
alone in the corner
no longer able to see or hear
what praise you have just spoke of him
held perfect as a daughter's love
given your readied hand
holding on for dear life
age three
to cross over
a scary street safe with you
makes crossing over
in the rain all the way over to Berkeley on Sunday morning
to celebrate the last
of her sweetheart George
just everything

My Autopsy

I know this will disappoint
when you know I know there are
seven stages of man
which I have already passed through
that his skin is replaced every seven years
which I have sloughed twelve times
and should know my insides out
but this is not a system review
I won't be specific for one reason
children are said to have landmarks
not stages to pass through
and we all are said to be children at heart
so begins the confusion how
senility begins at birth and goes on
to where I find myself with this contribution

what sustains us is the certainty
the next rung in life can't ever be as bad
as the one you have just passed through
which is true whatever level
you enter or better yet think you entered
the entropy journey
bearing in mind we all have to go through
the same process and you skip any mark at peril
of not having lived at all
better you hang in there
as the next stage is invariably worse
than what you have just been through

recall what scruff your daughter
brought into your kitchen for boyfriends
when you thought you'd completed
her preparation for the world
but hush my soul
no specificity here
all I want to leave you with is what
sustains us each step by step up the way is
how much more interesting
more amazing aging everything in life becomes
and that a sheen sparkles splendor on the edge
of every living thing
the closer you get
to whenever

Trapper John

In the darkness for a month
a white streak—months of streaks
at the glass patio door
always when you least expect
you're out gazing Virgo, Libra, Scorpio, Bear
he's there friendly confident
as all get out
passing by you
nose in the air
as if mustard gas
or is it phosgene makes you stand off
scared shitless he'll spray
the need to burn your clothes
bathe in tomato juice
best call the county trapper
a divot by the fence
that's it
he says
it's all access
they don't climb
a boiled egg peanut butter bread will do

cage rattle at midnight
from bed my wife cries out
is that it
is he dead
don't kill him
is he dead
his last meal peanut butter
this morning he's alive
he's mad fool
I took a close-up look for good measure
me one lucky mench

no spray
then went to the bookstore
Christmas gifts
for the children
when I returned
John smiled
he's gone
skunked
he's out of here
you enjoy your stars now Trapper said

How Are You

Everywhere I go
someones bent over a device working
this frenzy in thumbs
he doesn't see you
doesn't have to
he's got something in both ears
so he can't make you out anyway
he's already running away
and when he does call
it's when he has something else to do
he's in a movie line
on his way to the subway
on the eighteenth green
at a bar asking
can you hear me now
or stuck in traffic thinking
hey, this would be a good time to try them

come to think of it
we're all ancillary now
at a distance
dare ask
what happened to that call
every Sunday evening
exactly at six right as rain
to ask how are you
let you know
there have been no earthquakes
how much we love you
and the fun of learning firsthand
no one's in jail

Impaired

Not until I heard my loss
did I realize the swallow's song
this perfect October morning
comes from his love
for the sound of his own voice
and suddenly I wandered as I said farewell
for the last time
to my surgeon son
who is learning how to transplant
the human heart
from one dying to another living

did he sense my sadness in parting
the ineffable joyful
pride in my voice
as driving home
singing in the car
I discovered
I am no longer able to hear
the feelings I once could voice
so easily
in the songs I sing for myself

Betwixt

Where would I have been
if I had not been born right between
a boy and a girl
one their primogeniture prince
the other all that princess pink stuff
with Kipling's *If* for a headboard
here was I developing
a right brain and a left brain
all at once a survivor
hunkered down from crossfire
hardly even knowing
the heavenly preparation
I was getting
for the world of sensibility
by parents like all parents
you could never imagine having sex
anyway not with each other
maybe with a neighbor down the street
nevertheless planning some order
for children's arrival to the world
such that one caught in between
a first boy and a first girl
could turn out
inconceivably blessed
with benign neglect

Oneiric

I still dream of young women
they are generally healthy and have some quality
of someone I once knew many years before
my mind is subliminally filled with lust
while theirs always seems concerned with companionship
with getting to know how they love to talk
in long convoluted sentences
Jamesian paragraphs
like women will when they have you captive
driving somewhere in a car and you are trying
to read the morning paper with my oneiric ones
I find myself often selfishly directing conversation
to why it is 15 percent of young women
experts say are attracted to older men
not just the usual few years but disparate fatherly
even grandfatherly years
and mine do seem to say yes it's true
but not why I feel the way I do about you
as if that would be giving away a big secret

last night I dreamt of Emma
a graduate of the University of Texas who drawled sweetly
she didn't know till she was a senior you didn't
have to go to all them goddamn football games
which made us laugh and laugh

only this girl was much taller than Emma
the only resemblance as we lay there
next to each other in Lovers Park downtown
was a similarity of readied lips overwrought now
as if she had been excessively injected with Botox
she said all for me

Leisure

When I face this bright day
with nothing to do
the difficulty of doing nothing
that achievement
there is still that puzzle she is working on
down on the dining room table
the excitement of seeing
how much she has done beyond
where I left off last night
the Siamese cat paws are grasping toward
what I think will turn out to be worsted
even catnip of variegated colors
but enough is there to import a sense
of thrust pounce in a poised animal
of a thousand pieces
set onto some mortal ending
that could turn out to be nothing
but the least of which I can expect
will happen today

The Last Time

I stood on the old white porch alone
saying good-bye
to the country place we called Winding Water
for Mother who liked alliteration writ
on the station wagon door
me wrapped in my father's brown Burberry
the one I got him in London after the war
by merely giving a clerk his personal check
and I promised them both standing there alone
looking down across the terraces
covered in ice and snow
beyond where fertile green turf showed
through on the cold hillside
to the mill run waterfalls
and over to the sycamore
where rapids began with the secret channel
me and Ham could enter
with the wide flat-bottomed boat
and shoot all the way
downstream between the two islands
to the railroad bridge
over the Yellow Breeches
that if ever as now I am left the only one
of their four children
the Philadelphia bell will still call us to dinner
and the sound of the ripples
would be forever
the last living thing each night for me
before I too go to sleep

Animula

Animula vagula bland
hospes comesque corpori
quae nunc abibis in loca
pallidula rigida nudula
nec ut soles dabis iocus

My Soul

Little soul, lost and winsome
host companion for my life
pale, rickety, naked
you now seek another place
no longer joking at the race

Emperor Hadrian's famous last words
Trans JN

How to Listen

It will be all right if I die tonight
knowing I have taught
my four boys the trouble
they are having with their women
is that they think you are not listening
to them when they talk
as it is when they
talk to their women friends
with make them feel
exactly what they said
has been absorbed
and quietly masticated
even if it never is just certain
it ever is

Groundhog Day 1896

Today is my father's 116th birthday
each year this day now fifty years
since that day I couldn't get there
in time to keep him from getting out of bed
he still gets up and walks to his chambers
without so much as a word
looking down carefully
out of his one good eye
one step at a time
carefully avoiding the cracks in the red bricks
each bad line along the way
for the three blocks to the courthouse
and there this year over and over
as he struggles to climb slowly
up the marble steps
one by one at a time to himself
he repeats for each imperfect ascent
whether this nation
or any nation so conceived
can long endure

Waiting for Triple A

It's just you, but you are not alone.
Right now between Lubbock and Amarillo,
there's a guy out there pacing back and forth on
the highway who ruptured his oil pan on a stone.
He doesn't know it yet, but he burnt up
his motor driving a leak.
Picture the first-time woman
from out of town stalled sideways in traffic
in the Holland Tunnel.
She thinks it looks like a big
bathroom, which reminds her she has to go so
bad she can taste it.
But where? When? How long?
It's no help.
Just outside Elk, Nevada, there's a shit kicker's car
coughed to a stop right outside
the Muskrat Ranch.
He's on his way to his wife's delivery in Reno,
their sixth kid. The poor son of a bitch is running
a twelve million sperm count and wonders if there's time
to run across the street and get his ashes hauled before
his tow arrives. For the record he does. He gets his gun
with time to spare.
Back east outside Winchester Virginia,
a teenager tries to set the speed record for redheads,
Civil War General Phil Sheridan's classic
twenty-three-mile bareback ride to victory.
He gets out of his car, locks it,
and leaves the keys inside with the motor running.

Asshole.
But we've all done that. The hell of it is
if you haven't done that you haven't lived.
Yet there too like the radiator
that blew yesterday in Fruita, Utah
from oats bugs inspissated crossing free Kansas in July.
The kid has to go through the same exercise you do.
Just figure you're waiting.
Somewhere, somebody really gives a shit.
Maybe in West Palm Beach, an off-duty house dick would
interrupt his Philadelphia cheesesteak long enough
to make a call for you. There would be an immediate
response, a four-square, parchment-scrubbed, God-fearing
human being, a genuine sinner like you with answers. Not a
quadratic equation, a cascading algorithm to give Einstein
    jitters.

And help would come tout de suite and smile at you
because they care. And it would be a young married
couple with a beautiful child, gloriously happy.
And they would all walk upright.
They would know right off what was wrong and
know how and where to make it right.
And they would show how much they love you right off
because they could tell you were the kind of old man
who had made the same mistakes they are going through
and would fill up the rest of your life with their inexorable joy.

Age Three Remi Has to Go

I got the Pops duty again.
This time it's to be Home Depot.
She grabs my right index finger
and off we go, running pigeon-toed
through scissors and shades and hoses and fans.
We stop at planks and frames for directions.
"We get immer gerade aus YES tout doit."
"What did he say?" Remi asks.
"Go west," he says.
By the big stuff way back is
a woman stick figure door and a stick man door.
She goes for the woman door.
I redirect to the mens.
We pass three men facing up against the wall.
"What are they doing?" she asks.
"Hiding," I say.
"Hiding *what*?" she asks. "What do they have to hide?"
"They're hiding their membership," I say.
"What's membership?" she asks, her jeans already down,
jumping the seat before I can sanitize our world.
Father of boys, I can't be sure what's transpiring
as that quick she jumps off.
Nada.
No residue.

Some discoloration.
I give her four paper squares.
One by one, she waves the air fore and
aft for effect and hikes her jeans.
She puts her hands over her ears
at the same time she hits the flush bar with her elbow.
There's awful cascade.
We advance to washing.
Squeeze soap and run water.
Three new men appear against the wall.
Remi whispers as we leave, "They're hiding their
membership. What's membership?"
She's got to know.
"Ask your mother," I say.
So she does.
Her mother has her hands full of new kitchen appliances.
She explains how
if Remi is a good person when she grows up,
she too can have a membership at Home Depot
with nothing to hide.

Christmas 2011

I reminded them of the joy
when they were young
how the three used to fight and once
in the mountains in a snowstorm
Christmas Eve socked in
the middle one age three lacerated his right eyelid
scuffling on a table edge
I drove him ten miles in blinding slush
bleeding to the hospital
where they said he needed a plastic man
who'd take two hours in this mess to get there
and the nurses said it was immoral
against the law of privacy for me to do it
myself on my own family
they wouldn't give me anesthesia
and I said fuck you and grabbed
needle and thread
and the kid stared up at me in awe while I threw
twenty sweet instrument knots
cold turkey without a whimper
because he said it was interesting
to watch what I do
and he's the one who ended up in surgery you know
the one doing heart transplants

The Bouquet

At curtain call, we all lined up
one perfect line stage right to left
end-to-end smiling so as to show no hierarchy
and when the lead named Frank Hartley
who we called Hank Fartley
stepped forward for his solitary, triumphant bow
down the line I stepped forward too
to render myself equal
and afterward people
who didn't know any better
came upstage
and presented me with the roses
which is what I did
not yet center stage
as though I never would be
ever again

Pigeons

By the numbers they belong scrounging
the ledges above the entrance
to the New York Public Library
where they can anoint
you rushing in to be first in line to see
the rare book exhibit of Voltaire's *Candide*
or molting en masse the elms above your lunch
in the noisy park restaurant around the corner
when you have just been served your Reuben Sando
to find a big white dollop
center stage

but never here before
not where my astonishment
finds a solitary pair out my window
today in the meadow
lolling by the river in the Napa Valley
on a perfect morning
among our pristine egrets
and the new red-winged blackbirds
undaunted as clams
incongruously
two of them together
who got a life

Nurse Maria Theresa

To see you boxed in like that
in the empty church
and the man with the holy water
walking counterclockwise around you
in squeaky shoes from the wet floor
to be the only one who knew you
from the days when the Lock Company
had just converted back from making bullets for war
how us two together
nurse and doctor
cared for two thousand employees
the most any place in San Francisco
sick call three times a week
burns
lacerations
miscarriages
strokes
headaches
piles
unhappy mother-in-laws
the time the CEO set up his heart attack
the idea was to see if the young doctor
was sharp enough to diagnose a gold brick
you got wind of it the day before
warned me I came and made the CEO do push-ups

Marie sweetheart
dead age ninety
half of it for me
you are so much more
than twelve people there who didn't know you
a priest in squeaky dry shoes
walking on water
an empty church
you all boxed up there
us left out in the cold but once again at least
for a moment
our love together

Goosed

This mornin I swear
just as a jet blasted overhead to LA
a straggler announced his arrival
direct from Canada
circled me twice
over house over meadow
till he got clearance
then came in feet first
low over the sparkling pond
in the first good April sun
as tourists in a bright yellow Easter balloon
looked down in amazement
watching him close in over his perfect shadow
disappearing into a long slow landing glide
without a sound
or wake as he then stood up
there in triumph in the meadow
in the morning sun
looking up down and around
preening each wing once
in gratitude
to scream at me a fucking fico
take that

July 4

Hot air balloons crowd overhead
en masse
a giant flotilla
loaded with those who can't wait
to land
get down
get out
watch their morning collapse
and walk away downcast

where is the dazzle peaking
the fireworks on a hill above Dublin
joyously happy Jimmy Joyce
getting his gun
the sadder now
our washing up
once we're all done

Waiting For W. S. Merwin

I know if I behave
have enough patience
don't get my valence up
he will visit me twice a year
bring me something special
something like something
I already knew I had
even though I had not brought it
far enough for him
even though I may already have
one exactly like the one he brings me
and may even want to return it
to where I got it
but then I remember him as yesterday
how he waited tables on me in college
how he was never ever
good enough for promotion
so what appetite he has for me now
what he sets before me
is such astonishment
something so incomparably wrought
I can even taste his favorite aromas
a word rung true as life
the birdsong of a Maui morning
perfect

My Son The Surgeon

Three a.m. he calls me from the ER back east
says he wants me to keep my hand in
says this guy's got five stab wounds across
his chest—three left and one right one below sternum
says he's in shock and asks what he should do
I say run blood open left chest
says he did
the hearts stopped the sac full of blood
I say open that
says he did
five hundred cc blood and a hole in the heart
close that a whipped stitch
says he did that
says the heart's stopped
massage it
says he did that
it's fibrillating
shock it
zap it
says he did that
got regular beat
shock is bleeding elsewhere
so open right chest
says he did that
no bleeding
says blood running but still in shock
open abdomen
low sternum might be into liver
says he did that
no bleeding
only heart bleeding found

take to OR
says he did that
anesthesia delays for more blood
more lines running
give them hell
says he did that finally on table
too late
says that's right he died
right there on me
we could have saved him
cardiac tamponade only bleeding source
but the delay
yes delay
and the hell of it is it has happened before
and will happen again
anoxia
but Dad this guy was only nineteen
there is no poetry in this
no I say there is
no poetry
no poem son
keep good notes for the lawyers
I love you

The Bite

The long of it is the tongue
encased at ease
in a slithery recess cosseted against
the menace of teeth
quietly occupies itself
molding our fine discourse
turning a phrase
tasting our sweetest buds
for the high road
when one night over candlelight
with sudden chomp
the devil works his dance
on a fig
and a lover screams out bloody murder from her mouth
split and forked
with a *lingua diaboli*
bleeding and smiling
his deadly scar upon our life

Young Lovers

I only meant to say
how you now know yourself
is not just nothing of what
will become of you
but that it is there for you
not so much to go forward with
when what will come
overcomes you
with what you don't expect
as it is the ingredients
of everything there will be
out there for you
and what you thinks
enough for you now
to carry you on to
wherever you are thinking
to go on to next
still needs much more of
what I know to be
the same you

Breakfast Nook

A shot from the blind in the meadow
a white bird wobbles helpless
a flight careens
crashes in my patio
just as the doorbell rings
the realtor lady
her early appointment to sell the house
I grab two hot pads
rush outside
the animal is in agony
a magnificent white barn owl
convulsing blood
heart rate a thousand a minute
gasping
doll's eyes rolling up
dying

I grasp him with hot pads
heave him way over the back fence
no dead weight
hollow bird bones
how still they still fly
into the high chaparral
the doorbell rings twice
a third time urgent

I rush to the door
welcome her smiling face
she wanders in
looks around
sees my dishes
says what a great place, a nice nook like this, is
to have breakfast
sit here
read the papers
your buyers will love it
and the view
so quiet a place like this
to start the day
it's a go
a piece of cake

Reservatus

If you can make a point to her
without so much as a word
that she always should be more
excited about what
she thinks you are up to
than where you are at
even when what you are doing
is nothing more than
what you might think
anyone else in the same boat
would want to wait around
to do for her
your whole world of endless
waiting on her
while she nips into
the pharmacy
and runs into someone
she says she hasn't seen
for at least three weeks
will change in a flash of urge
one night
as getting it just right
without having to play catch up
your life will never come to hearing
being on time
is a just waste of time
for both of you ever
again

Blocked

If you can't recall the first name
the first name overnight
of Steve Kaufman
who had sweet baby hair growing out his ears
for that matter
if you forgot anyone's by now
just forget it
then when it's furnaced enough
a time you won't expect
like to the lark at break of day
arising from sullen earth
the morning crush
blocked above San Rafael
before the bridge
will suddenly clear
break free
a synapse kick in
zooming forth astonishment
and suddenly you're hit suddenly
with *hey*
it's *Steve*

Stymie

He came at me quickstep
on the narrow path
with a bob and weave
a head fake left
so I moved to the right
but he was there
then to left
there too
then both of us danced
right left right
left right left
stymied
he with a boutonniere
me in my sweats
froze in place
no joy nor gratitude
for the contact
the impasse
while even ants know
always best
to kindly touch antennae
then graciously move along

Reunions

One day you wake up
you realize seven years have passed
your cells have all turned over
your skin has changed
your surface
fresh and new
you set forth to greet your friends
who have all new cells
new smiles
a resumptive fragrance
then one shows up you always
couldn't stand
he looks better
until it hits you
suddenly you can't forgive or forget
you talk
it's hopeless
it all comes back
you wonder why that is
why don't we speak
like we're told we should
but this is visceral
from within
from way back
ineducable
won't change anything
and born with the same
immutable sadness
as sex

Class Notes
For George Cahill

Time comes when no longer
the names are those you know
moving through these pages
where those now
appear doing nothing
that you have not already done
and none of the names you do know
that still land here
are not those you once were sure about
as it was always easier to live with certainty
among all the others
who come and go that this one
or especially that one in truth
for the life of me
would live forever

Fetal

In her sun basket
by the window
celebrating twenty-two and a half years
she circles
closes her eyes
and curls up just so
in the brightness
configured perfect
without giving a thought
to hunch up her legs
tuck in her chin
fold her arms
and suspend herself
in darkness
where we all are
and once were
and still remain
gathered together
at last
in sleep

Doing the Math 2012

Today, I am eighty-six years old. In 1936, when I was ten, my father took me to see Babe Ruth hit a home run down the right field line at Griffith's Stadium in Washington, DC. Ruth was forty-one. He waddled to first base where they put in a substitute runner to complete the bases for him. You can't do that anymore. That summer, Daddy was Ruth's age. He took me to the Last Encampment at Gettysburg, where there were thousands of pup tents for the last veterans of Pickett's Charge. My father sat me on a cannon and recited Lincoln's address in tears. You can still cry there. But can boys sit on cannons? One old rebel said he was eighty-six, born in 1850. He had been a drummer boy with Pettigrew's Division, age thirteen. He said his father, when he was my age ten, had known George Washington in Virginia in 1795. I'll tell my grandchildren today how I once knew a man whose father knew George Washington. They'll freak in amazement. I'll let them all do the math.

My Jeremy

We two once had our hour mornings
I could throw my cover
spring alert
jump so high
a Giverny frog en soleil
off a lily pad dripping
to start the day
irrepressible in the buff
en plain air
to the heavens on high
I would leap pirouettes
all the way to the tub
to the children's delight
with their big belly laughs
they'd clap and cheer
they'd scream and yell
for more of me
au naturel
until my first gave it the hook
proclaimed the tallywacker
worse than shook
worse than uncouth
worse than Socrates himself
corrupting our youth
came out of her mouth
she shot me down
ours a short run
when me and my Jeremy Frog
were one

Eulogy
For Molly C

In the morning
she'd pounce my chest
making biscuits on my breasts

Sleeping Alone

Given enough time I promise
the grandfather clock down the hall
from your mother will no longer
strike you at night
and whimpers long next you
will anchor another room
the amazement of another morning
will be born in company
how all leave this world alone
gets rehearsed every night
when we wake to discover
the miracle sun still shining
through the slats
bright across the river
how you have slept once again
all night through
without a piss call
dreaming young women
the ones who reproduce
who own the only one
good reason left not to sleep without some body
who will help you lift and tug and spring alert
to suspend the branches of the old Japanese elm
with red and blue bungee cords
first thing this morning
high above the terrace wall
to give everybody coming
just the right shade of shade to pretend to smile
for your last going-away party
again today

Dream House

I built her our house in springtime
right where she chose
right by the water's edge
where the ebb and flood brought driftwood
wonderfully sculpted
where the children grew cherry brown
strong running our beach
chasing muscles worth eating
orange anemones that closed completely
over the toes for fun
in fall I would sail my Laser #7
to the lowing sun
my favorite time of year
watch her throw pots
beneath the overarching oak that sprinkled gold leafs
in her long black hair
I hardly noticed the change
I never wanted it to
insidious happens so gradual

but winter did come
you sat in a corner
without a word you said
there was more to life
than old driftwood
than children growing brown and strong for life
even more than love
by the water's edge

Aliquot

The truth must dazzle gradually
Or every man be blind
    Emily Dickinson

If you grasp and pull your seat belt
too fast just to rush the ice cream home
before it melts in the noonday sun
it sticks and jerks won't let you go
unless you slow down
drag it out
slowly like a romance insinuated over
time in aliquots of sweetness
where gradually it secures a place
of love you always intended
and finally gets going for you
all locked in both just
one loving bundle
ready to ride
together

Stoplight

The corner red light
makes people stop and go
without listening
all daylight long

after dinner the glare
blinks red and black
shadow boxing the TV
in the living room

until midnight when
they turn her into
a steady yellow stream
the sirens can scream past
unimpeded

in the city
where we live
love and sleep
deprived

My Ocular Migraine

Like northern lights
no one knows anything about
this comes out of the blue
without a swatch of pain
in a galaxy of French sparklers
running cups and saucer lightning
blinding your mind's eye
it takes over the realm
a light show
the kind you wait all day
to take the kids to ten p.m. at Disneyland
where any moment
there's nothing but glittering skittering
dark spots all over

and I'm lost
stopped
left no place to go
twenty minutes more or less
in a blind
scattered Dantean darkness
till a force comes and helps
gather me away
as if you just rubbed
rebarbative wake-up from your eyes
leaving me alive
alone
to what where and when will it be again

Afterword

If only I knew where
they come from
knowing only
that each one is something
before it is about something
you have to know about
a thing
that needs an allowance
to run itself down
that interrupts something
I was doing
like taxes today
then of all things
imagine how
lost for amazement
gathering without this poem
without so much as a word
it would be
not to discover what
this turns out to be
at last
and afterward